NORRIS

THE BEST OF
NORRIS

McClelland and Stewart

McClelland and Stewart Limited
The Canadian Publishers
25 Hollinger Road
Toronto, Ontario
M4B 3G2

Canadian Cataloguing in Publication Data

Norris, Len, 1913-
    The best of Norris

ISBN 0-7710-6820-4

1. Canadian wit and humor, Pictorial.* I. Title.

| NC1449.N6A4 1984 | 741.5′971 | C84-098990-3 |

Printed and bound in Canada

INTRODUCTION

Most people will agree that pictures are among the simplest forms of communication. Most of us drew pictures before we could write words. This is a book of simple pictures designed to communicate. Some might enlighten; some just remind; some merely assure you of company in your opinion. Some stir protest. None, I hope, preach. Once in a while some might commiserate.

These cartoons have been culled from a vast lode I have been accumulating at the rate of about five a week for thirty years. (Incidentally, you might notice from the cartoons that history does indeed repeat itself.)

Thirty years ago these particular editorial cartoons were a bit odd. "Editorial cartoons" in most papers were "political cartoons," and in North America they followed a pattern of symbolized figures (Uncle Sam, Jack Canuck, etc.) and caricatures of political leaders with well-labelled accessories like "TAX AXE," "GRAFT BAG," etc. My efforts with these "traditional" editorial cartoons were dismal to awful and fortunately few. I soon decided to do what came naturally, and my drawings began to reflect the region that I lived in, and the reactions of my neighbours and friends to political events became editorial comment. I didn't invent the style – it was, and still is, used by a number of cartoonists in Europe and Britain, such as Strube, Giles, Trog etc. – but I believe I was the first in Canada to use it. And Vancouver, West Vancouver, and Victoria were made-to-order stage settings.

I was a lot more at ease as a social commentator than as a political pundit. There are few things in the world and fewer in politics that can be analyzed and explained with black lines drawn in a 6″ x 7″ (unmetricated) white rectangle – daily. Certainly I can't do it. But, like my neighbours, I can react quite quickly to the *effect* of events – either anticipated or feared or felt immediately – without having to explain the technical details of cause. And I could do this to a daily deadline.

This simple communication allows the addition of the other important ingredient in my book – the light touch. The day-by-day shenanigans of government waste, new taxes, unemployment figures, and so on, don't lend themselves to side-splitting mirth, but bitter pills do slide down a little better with a coating of whimsy.

Because the events some of these cartoons refer to may have occurred back beyond ken or memory, a few explanatory notes have been added to some from the three earlier decades. Without these, today's reader may wonder what the fuss – over a glass of wine at a tea shop, or a postage stamp increase to six cents – is all about.

And finally, I happen to think of a cartoon as a piece of art work – not as a dashed-off sketch. It must have composition (particularly if it's "busy," as many of mine are), and the perspective and the anatomy should be correct. Proper animation, an individual style, and careful drawing mark the professional. It helps, too, if the drawings present a good idea.

Please don't ask me to explain how to get these.

(December 12, 1951)

Canada's Undefended Border

"You new on the job?"

"Filbert Phelps!"

(March 24, 1952)

(May 29, 1952)

"One thing before we go in—we found it advisable in Alberta not to wear our halos at a rakish angle..."

"...the question is...do goose pimples tan?"

(June 24, 1952)

At the time I drew this cartoon, the United States was seeing a Communist under every bed, and many highly visible Hollywood personalities were being quite vocal in their political philosophies. Charlie Chaplin, the most prominent comedian in the world, was refused entry to the United States and banished to England, much to the dismay of his many fans, who would not have cared if his politics were radical Hottentot.

"…Born? Where you going? For how long?…Ever laugh at Charlie Chaplin?"

(September 27, 1952)

"If this is what goes on in the day schools...what must it be like at Night School...?"

Reggie is the earliest incarnation of my redneck radical arch-conservative. He evolved over the years into Rodney, who appeared much more regularly.

(October 1, 1953)

"What really puts Reggie out of sorts is their constant reference to some footling rounders game between New York and one of its suburbs as a 'World Series'."

"*Rodney, do you suppose this gentleman might happen to know if it will be one, or two trains a day…?*"

Sharp eyes might have spotted the missing chair without being told, but I doubt it. I forgot to ink in the chair or I did it on purpose because I drew it on April Fool's Day. I forget. Not that it mattered; nobody – to my knowledge – noticed.

"Trouble is…what'll we think of next…?"

The letters PGE stand for Pacific Great Eastern Railway, fondly known as the Please Go Easy Railway, amongst other things. It's now called the B.C. Railway. It had been abandoned before I came to West Vancouver in 1950. Locals had incorporated the right-of-way into their gardens, planting wallflowers, scarlet runners, patio sets, croquet pitches, etc., on it. Sudden talk of its revival brought shocked disbelief and utter consternation to horrified natives and provided me with dozens of cartoons.

(May 17, 1954)

Resolved, by the West Van Beautification and Adoration Society...that if the PGE is inevitable, it be made to conform to the local surroundings...

"…and if, through the medium of this great sport, we have contributed to the betterment of international relations and understanding, then we are indeed amply rewarded…"

"We got along without this fluoridation, or teeth, in my day..."

THE VANCOUVER SUN

(March 30, 1955)

NEWS ITEM: NUDISTS TO BUILD OWN SUBDIVISION HERE

THE VANCOUVER SUN

(July 19, 1955)

"Sometimes I suspect Figsby of not being sincere..."

(July 20, 1955)

"Nothing, of course, will ever convince Rodney that they'll go through with their ridiculous plans to build the railway…"

Artist's conception of wild west gunman's holdup of Victoria's Empress Hotel, reconstructed from all available data and eyewitness accounts…

(September 27, 1956)

"Actually I came last year to learn to fix a leaky tap, and stayed on to make my fortune..."

"...What's all this tom fool talk about a school for accident-prone drivers...?"

A sidestep in Reggie's evolution into Rodney: momentarily, he becomes Sidney.

"…and the very moment we switched it on, it insulted Sidney's intelligence…"

(December 4, 1956)

"…and I'd like to see just one report of something that went down…"

"Children…have you forgotten our little plan to approach the Canada Council?"

(June 1, 1957)

(July 13, 1957)

"What...and let all the flowers die...!"

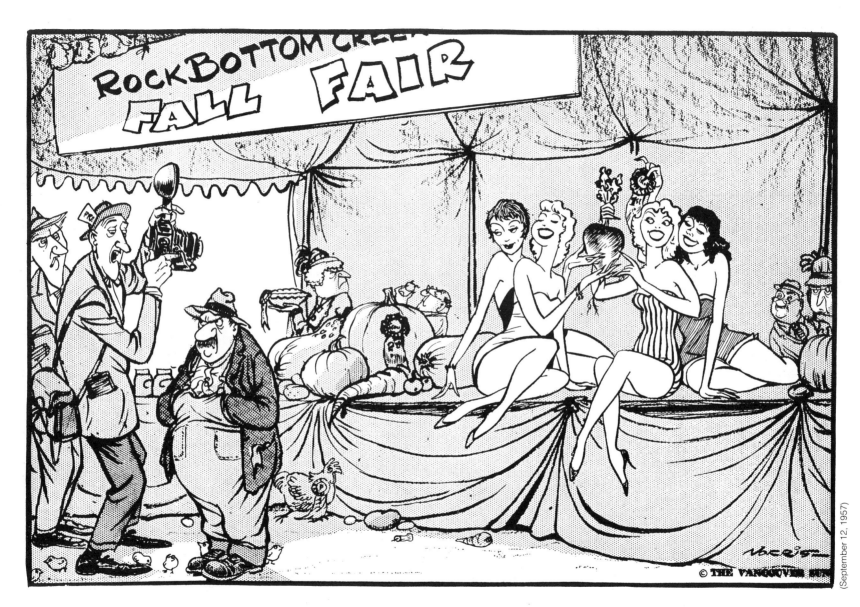

(September 12, 1957)

"OK, so you grew the prize turnip….D'you want to get its picture in the paper or don'tcha…?"

NEWS ITEM: PROBE BEGINS AS P.G.E. TRAIN REFUSES TO STOP FOR PASSENGERS

''…They'll just have to make up their minds…trains running on time, or footling around in
stations picking up passengers…'''

(January 28, 1958)

@ THE VANCOUVER SUN

"Drive the bus, call the stops, make change, sell tickets, keep on schedule...now this!"

"All very well...but how would you like your daughter marrying a Liberal...?"

© THE VANCOUVER SUN

(May 10, 1958)

"*Listen, B.C. Electric, you put my rates up again and I take my business some place .... else...*"

NORRIS
THE VANCOUVER SUN

(July 19, 1958)

The Sons of Freedom are a radical sect of Doukhobors given to burning most things and bombing the rest in attempts to get their way. They were active in British Columbia's Kootenay District at this time and were much seen in the news for their habit of taking off all their clothes at the drop of a hat. The Victoria Conservative Club is my name for the Union Club of Victoria, a proper gentleman's club founded in 1879. I use it freely and often as the hangout of Fotheringay, an unblushing clone of David Low's Colonel Blimp.

VICTORIA CONSERVATIVE CLUB

FREEDOMITE DOUKS THREATEN TO EMBARRASS GOVT.

© THE VANCOUVER SUN

(August 19, 1958)

"...on second thought, Fotheringay's suggestion that it's a jolly good idea if we also embarrass the government, has been discarded as undignified..."

"D'you realize, when we unload this lot we can afford the ones in the cans…?"

(September 5, 1958)

"...Can't help that...if it's livin', it's either a dependent or a taxpayer..."

(December 13, 1958)

"...That does it, madam...second kid today not housebroken..."

(January 29, 1959)

"Studley…I understand you are falling behind on two of your majors…fees and board…"

(February 13, 1959)

"*…and when we go to all the trouble of giving you even more waiting time I suppose you still won't have it ready.*"

"Licensed and leashed."

(March 17, 1959)

(March 26, 1959)

"...an utterly beastly suggestion, obviously spawned on the Continent and proposed by some cad who's never heard of the word cricket."

"Sidney, you come right in before you catch your death of strontium 90!"

(April 3, 1959)

NEWS ITEM: CANADIAN MILITIA TO TURN IN WEAPONS

© THE VANCOUVER SUN

(May 6, 1959)

"…42nd Tiddlycove Boy Scout Troop, now the most heavily armed group in the area."

(August 18, 1959)

"OK, dear…drive me to drink…"

THE VANCOUVER SUN (December 31, 1959)

"They start messing about with the organization and it will end up in chaos."

"Let the premier tell me when he's havin' his blinkin' election and then I'll tell you if I'm Gina Lollabrigida or not."

(March 10, 1960)

"...an invitation to the program Candlelight and Wine...with the sparkle of crystal and the gleam of fine silver we offer a quiet background to add pleasure to the elegance of dining..."

(April 23, 1960)

"*Just as I thought…clogged with money again.*"

(May 11, 1960)

In the early days of anti-smoking campaigns, Barry Mather, a columnist and later an MP, was a prime mover. That's him on stage. Dedicated smoker Norris remained a skeptic and a scoffer until a major hospital visit a couple of years ago, which produced rapid reform.

June 23, 1960)

"Chocolate! Chewing gum! Peanuts! Popcorn!..."

(July 7, 1960)

Believe it or not, lotteries used to be not only illegal in Canada, they were considered immoral. Everyone bought (under the counter) Irish Sweepstakes tickets – to help the hospitals, of course.

(October 22, 1960)

THE VANCOUVER SUN

"…found in possession of three Irish Sweep Tickets, one George Phelps, alias 'Fat Chance', alias 'Lucky This Time', alias 'Need You Now'…"

One of a popular series of annual office Christmas party cartoons.
These suffered a gradual demise as the crackdown on drinking
drivers hardened.

"….and a vote of thanks to Mr. Redside, our comptroller, who was in charge of decorations this year…"

(December 23, 1960)

"As a matter of fact, I was really trying to find the provincial welfare department..."

"By the way…in the event it sinks, is Sidney obligated to go down with the ship?"

(February 9, 1961)

(May 31, 1961)

"Sidney!—Elbows off the table!"

"Ethel! What d'we earn this week...outside the hundred-forty thou' on the Irish Sweep?"

THE VANCOUVER SUN

(June 3, 1961)

"This the deep or shallow end?"

THE VANCOUVER SUN

(July 13, 1961)

A spate of book censorship hit Victoria. Pornography seemed to lurk in every publication included in the school curriculum and in all of the books in the public libraries. The Social Credit government of the day attracted some righteous and diligent bluestockings, perhaps a legacy of the original true-blue Socreds.

THE VANCOUVER SUN

(October 17, 1961)

"...do you wish to exercise your search warrant...or join the library and let me find it for you?"

(December 9, 1961)

"...We feel confident in assuring you, madam, that the possibility of the child achieving nuclear fission
with the junior set is quite remote."

"PHILATELISTS!"

THE VANCOUVER SUN

(January 12, 1962)

"Same old stuff and nonsense...in my day it was 'stunts your growth.'"

THE VANCOUVER SUN

(April 5, 1962)

"What a paradise, Sidney...only one little cloud in the sky."

"What say we put the blame where it belongs...on the government's new high interest rates."

THE VANCOUVER SUN

(July 7, 1962)

(September 8, 1962)

"...What's more, I want you to pick a trade you'll be proud to go on strike from."

(November 3, 1962)

"...could you suggest one that might give our Amblesnide and Tiddlycove Hike and Tramp Club a more positive sense of purpose...?"

(March 6, 1963)

*"The Red Cross, sir, and I took the liberty of saying you would be delighted to donate your usual, sir
...a pint of money."*

"My George wouldn't dream of depriving our country's leaders of the full benefit of his advice…"

(April 2, 1963)

"Pinched? Who by?"

(April 13, 1963)

"*Of course I remember you, Mrs. Terseleigh. Last Easter you wore a saucy straw cloche dramatically accented with tulle roses in striking spring taupe…*"

"...a hale and healthy worm, Mrs. Phelps, is living proof of the complete absence of dangerous insecticides..."

(September 10, 1963)

"Rodney will be simply furious if it puts him into a higher tax bracket."

"I loved this part, didn't you?"

"….then, on a pre-arranged signal…"

(December 19, 1963)

"It's the premier…promises to wish us 'Christmas,' in writing, if the federal government and city
will supply the 'A' and the 'Merry'…"

(March 19, 1964)

"...Rodney! Does this mean we will be able to take it with us?"

"What! Another increase in the cost of gracious living?"

(March 25, 1964)

Paul Hellyer's plan to merge the Canadian armed forces brought wrathful comments from flotillas of retired admirals in Nanaimo and Victoria – and put my imagination to work.

"What's more, Phelps, there has been no suggestion to merge the services within the Scout movement."

Early on, the flag debate drew avid disinterest, except for a plaintive
wail or two from dyed-in-the-wool traditionalists (like me).

(May 15, 1964)

"When did you last wave a flag?"

"Air Canada, hello? Leave does when the flight Toronto to?"

(June 2, 1964)

In 1954, the B.C. Lions football team was started. Ten years later a packed stadium still gave standing ovations for a first down. Meanwhile the more rabid monarchists were at Brockton Oval watching cricket – and the grass grow.

(September 26, 1964)

"Come on, roar, you B.C.s, roar! Wallop Yorkshire with a score! From the mountains to the sea! Show 'em cricket in B.C.! Rah! Rah! Rah!"

"...you don't see Red Ensigns muckin' up the lawns like this."

(October 3, 1964)

THE VANCOUVER SUN

(November 28, 1964)

(December 8, 1964)

"Accosting strangers…soliciting…incoherent speech…"

"Rodney is forming a band of merry men, dressed in forest green, camped in a woodland glade..."

(January 8, 1965)

Early separatist talk from Quebec drew mild interest in British Columbia at the time, but I offered a sympathetic gesture of help anyway.

"We'd adore motoring through Quebec...doing our bit, so to speak, to knit Confederation."

THE VANCOUVER SUN (May 14, 1965)

NEWS ITEM: MERGER OF ANGLICAN AND UNITED CHURCHES NEAR

THE VANCOUVER SUN ©

(June 2, 1965)

"Let's face it...it's going to take some effort for us to stop feeling holier than thou."

(June 18, 1965)

"...you don't look like a Commonwealth prime minister to me, mate."

The year 1966 marked the Great Lotteries Crackdown to save the country from moral ruin. The Crackdown may have occurred because the Irish, and not the government moralists, ran the only game in town.

NEWS ITEM: POLICE OFFICIALS AND DETECTIVES PRESS IRISH SWEEPSTAKES ROUNDUP.

THE VANCOUVER SUN

(January 5, 1966)

"Now this is what we're after, men...the nom de plume will be different, of course. Mine just happens to be 'Cop-it-Lucky'."

"Then it's settled. We model ourselves on Canada and use a four-party system."

"... before I could tell 'em it was a busted water main, they'd unanimously approved it as the Centennial Fountain."

(March 3, 1966)

(March 18, 1966)

"Out!"

It was decreed that henceforth the Civil Service would be bilingual. He had to communicate like this, didn't he?

"Darling, I am just a poor civil servant…cheri, je ne suis qu'un pauvre fonctionnaire…but I love you…mais je vous aime beaucoup…will you…voulez-vous…"

"...and Rodney is so terribly sensitive and concerned about the happiness and future well-being of his fellow man...particularly as it affects the market..."

(May 13, 1966)

"...other than that, did the union have a nice meeting?"

"...having studied our governments' welfare, pension and taxation plans, and being of sound mind...
I spent the whole damn lot in the last week."

(September 17, 1966)

(September 28, 1966)

"*...our great problem in B.C., Your Grace, is the widespread local belief that this is Heaven...*"

"…dunno, bo'sun, all I asked the Admiral was if it was OK now to call the bow the front, the deck the floor, starboard the right and…"

(March 21, 1967)

"*Our achievement award this month to Harry Gallspiel…for finding 14 loopholes in the Consumer Protection Act…*"

"He's now a teaching assistant...and while he doesn't actually run the university..."

(March 22, 1967)

(June 8, 1967)

"Just the spectators, Addlewitz...the spectators..."

"Rodney actually started appreciating modern art the day he found the whole world to be incomprehensible."

(November 23, 1967)

"Now, wasn't that just as good as Paris?...peculiar natives, sidewalk tables, our French-language radio station turned on...a glass of local wine..."

Nine and a quarter per cent for a fifteen- to twenty-year mortgage was massive! This was before we got used to cheering when the mortgage rate dropped a tenth of a point to 18 per cent.

(March 30, 1968)

"Well, not really. We got talking about the 9¼% mortgage..."

"*…as Rodney so aptly put it, mere words simply cannot do justice in describing the magnificent Festival ballet…*"

(July 5, 1968)

"Do I criticize your hobby?"

(August 17, 1968)

There was loud complaint when the price of postage stamps leapt from five cents to six cents. (Well, it *was* a 20 per cent increase.)

"RSVP! Do they think I'm made of money?"

GOVT DROPS
WINTER WORK
PROGRAM
ECONOMY
MOVE

NORRIS
THE VANCOUVER SUN

(September 6, 1968)

"I suppose there will be cries of outrage from the places that have winter..."

(October 24, 1968)

"You mean you didn't notice that new deal of total tax exemption of gifts between spouses?"

(November 27, 1968)

"…What bugs me is which one of them knew how to spell 'ultimatum'."

"*It's only* vin du pays…*we're a bit strapped as Cecil is between Canada Council grants.*"

"...we are advised to accept their expropriation offer or submit, within a period of three days, to appropriate independent appraisal..."

(February 20, 1969)

(February 28, 1969)

"A five cent stamp please...I'm boycotting the six cent one because of the poor mail service."

NORRIS
THE VANCOUVER SUN

(June 10, 1969)

"Personnel department? Would you please clarify by memo the summer job you hired one
William P. Flotsome, student, first year arts, SFU, to perform..."

(July 8, 1969)

"*...can I help it if you're for free enterprise and I'm for state socialism?*"

"Think of me, if you will, as a shopping centre in your midst with no bad zoning, traffic, environmental or deteriorated property value side effects…"

(October 3, 1969)

"I'd like half a pound of anything you have that doesn't contain tars, resins, pesticide residues, polysuper-saturated fats, artificial sweeteners, softeners, foaming agents or chemical additives..."

(October 23, 1969)

"You're aware, I suppose, that money is a poor choice due to the rapid depreciation factor…"

(November 25, 1969)

(December 4, 1969)

"Actually, I'd just like to pop in once a day and get my own mail delivered..."

(December 31, 1969)

''We always drink and drive...''

"...actually, a Croix de Guerre was flushed down it."

Rodney the Redneck at full voice and prepared to make
one of his typical arrangements for René Lévesque.

(May 21, 1970)

*"I know what I'd tell Quebec...the Plains of Abraham are still there and I'll even make it best
two out of three."*

"She's on a visit, he's on strike, they're on holiday, I'm on tranquilizers..."

(June 30, 1970)

(August 26, 1970)

"*...surely we can work out some mutually agreeable means of friendly pollution of the Arctic.*"

(November 3, 1970)

"I wonder if they realize that yielding our heraldic traditions and symbols to appease Quebec changes Rodney Couchant to Rodney Rampant?"

(December 2, 1970)

"Burglar? How d'you know it isn't just some Ottawa civil servant taking from the rich to give to the poor?"

DAVEY REPORT
500000 WORD
CRITIQUE OF
MEDIA

(December 12, 1970)

"Actually…Rodney has said it all in letters to the editor."

"I suppose you realize, plugging this lot in probably foreshadows the flooding of another beautiful Canadian wilderness valley."

(December 22, 1970)

"I trust you are not corrupting young minds by circumventing official standards of Canadian content in your repertoire."

(January 26, 1971)

(January 27, 1971)

"*Think of yourself as a Canada Development Corporation, dedicated to keeping 50 feet of your country in Canadian hands…*"

"...he had just dropped in his income tax when along came the paper boy..."

"What do you expect...with them taxing all gains except ill-gotten."

"Fat lot of thanks I seem to be getting for an all-out effort to solve the international balance of payments fiasco."

(October 2, 1971)

(November 10, 1971)

"Maybe this is the big year...when schools price themselves out of the market."

(November 16, 1971)

"As I understand Rodney's explanation of the guaranteed annual income plan, everyone else, if the need arose, could clip his coupons..."

"I know everything goes by air...what puzzles me is how do you get your airplanes to stay in the air at five miles an hour?"

(January 5, 1972)

(February 5, 1972)

"He's at that awkward age...too young for old age security, too old for Opportunities for Youth, too late for family allowance, too conventional for Canada Council or local initiative programs, too poor for tax loopholes, too rich for subsidized housing..."

"Actually, we thought Fred was unemployed...then he was seasonally adjusted..."

(October 11, 1972)

"I said...we were one of the lucky ones...not expropriated for airport expansion."

(February 1, 1973)

"...good news, Ethel...Ethel..."

(March 23, 1973)

"Frankly...I just can't see them going for this outfit."

"...what's become of good old caveat emptor?"

"All very well...but what've you done about the cost of meat?"

(July 11, 1973)

"*I don't think you should expect wondrous things from the federal-provincial conference on Western Economic Opportunities overnight...*"

"Rodney was advised that the best hedge against inflation was to purchase art, Persian rugs or wine..."

"Tennis anyone...?"

"So nothing came of them again this year...you'll cheer up when your government tomato crop failure subsidy cheque comes."

(October 2, 1973)

(November 24, 1973)

"*Gosh, we've been practising conservation and restraint for all the wrong reasons…poverty.*"

(January 25, 1974)

''*This year, in the spirit of national equalization, Reggie and I feel we should spend our vacation in the have-not provinces…*''

"…why can't we have a retirement savings plan that doesn't require burning down the house?"

(February 19, 1974)

"I don't have a public opinion."

(June 25, 1974)

(August 31, 1974)

"It's Alfred's idea to take a leaf from hockey's book...add a bit of body contact, the odd fight, turn pro and pick up a hundred thousand or so a year."

(September 13, 1974)

"It started out as his report under the Public Officials Disclosure Act, but now he's thinking in terms of a snappy title, hard cover, movie rights..."

"I have a LIP grant to do kidney research..."

"Your final demand...double or nothing...has intriguing aspects that management would like to study."

"...problem with giving lands back to the Indian and Eskimo peoples...leaves the CPR owning all the rest."

"*This year, in the spirit of conservation of energy, Roger has them blink on and off.*"

(December 17, 1974).

(February 13, 1975)

"*I must confess to feeling some trepidation over our government's meddling in percentages of Canadian content in our reading matter.*"

"I'd like to report three housing starts...we got a start when we learned the price...another start when we heard the mortgage interest...and an awful start when we saw the property tax."

(May 8, 1975)

"Multinational oil companies handing out millions in bribes around the world and what does he accept for doing business with them? A tumbler."

(May 21, 1975)

"Oh, another beautiful new stamp...I do hope you find one that works soon."

(June 11, 1975)

(July 15, 1975)

"At the moment ma'am, I don't think there's any law against painting the nude martini glass…however, should the martini itself be present…"

"You shouldn't get excited about your one little blue suitcase, ma'am...did you know we plan to lose 25 million of your bucks this year?"

(August 2, 1975)

"*...regardless of that Miss Speling, 15 months service as a government secretary does not carry automatic appointment to the Senate.*"

(August 21, 1975)

"...and as if we don't have enough problems already, we're going to have to teach them to give litres instead of quarts..."

(August 23, 1975)

"...all right then...here it is in English..."

(December 19, 1975)

"May I see a shirt, not artificially overpriced by government decree or subsidized from the public purse, and of such vile design and fit to provide the minimum of anguish when the tax departments demand it?"

THE VANCOUVER SUN

(April 21, 1976)

"Count y'change ma'am...we're 900 million short and Casey here could be trying to make it up."

"As an Opposition critic I would be remiss if I didn't sum up the budget with one cute derogatory phrase..."

(May 26, 1976)

"The highlight of the games...one more time Ethel and her name will come to me..."

(July 31, 1976)

"When?...ah, that's for me to know and you to find out."

(September 3, 1976)

"Did I tell you? Sidney likes to celebrate Labor Day with a militant display of belligerency."

(September 4, 1976)

"The latest poll shows one person in four likes the government...so which one of you is it?"

(September 8, 1976)

"When I say damn the salmon fishing...it's not the same as when Hydro says it."

(September 22, 1976)

"Ethel, did you cause to be sold, via St. Swiffin's rummage sale, one half pound of produce, to wit, your tomatoes?"

(February 15, 1977)

"I say forming a monastery and becoming monks is a small price to pay for upgrading the prestige of the product and getting the jump on local competition..."

"...Mother's making another futile gesture."

(October 7, 1977)

"I don't think a man who shares $8 billion in debt with his government can be called a
conservative, unimaginative piker...."

"Of course, being in government, Sylvester prefers to celebrate Thankstaking"

(October 8, 1977)

"...on the other hand, you carry on without the glare of controversy and publicity."

(November 30, 1977)

"Can't help that...starting Monday the building industry goes metric...which is when I plan to hang them 33-centimetre doors on them 16-inch cabinets...."

(December 30, 1977)

"....I think they'd appreciate it if you and I, Rodney, were to just pop in to say bonjour...."

"Y'know, they used to turn him down for Canada Council grants...then he started putting those words in his poems."

(May 2, 1978)

"...of course, medically speaking, swapping an entire wife...."

(July 13, 1978)

"...do you recall the price of a gallon of petrol when we had Lawrence of Arabia in charge?"

"Could you pop back later...they're at the movies."

(August 25, 1978)

"I realize these days it is only money, Miss Debbett, but in the interest of tidiness, could we try not to spill?"

(September 30, 1978)

"Of course they didn't put a stamp on it... who'd have thought it would get delivered?"

"...dare one hope that it also presages renewed strong international demand for the Canadian dollar?"

"The experts predicted the world would run out of gas in 20 years...but they forgot your father."

(July 17, 1979)

"Beset by this crisis…people should try to take no unnecessary trips, use car pools or public transportation whenever you can, park your car one extra day per week, obey the speed limit, and set your thermostats to save fuel…there is absolutely no way to avoid sacrifice." – President Carter

"…dare I hope that you are not counted among the 60,000 civil servants slated for dismissal."

"*...next, I'll work out the total interest over the 25-year mortgage, which may cause you some raised eyebrows....*"

(October 3, 1979)

"…and we know, in this era of dirty tricks, that our party's straight-from-the-shoulder method in placing issues squarely before you will elicit a warm response…."

(October 20, 1979)

(November 22, 1979)

"So far, you're in luck…location of 'men's' is not classified under national security…."

"On the other hand, in this day and age can one look askance when one is blessed with a surplus…?"

"What really bugs him is being utterly ignored by Greenpeace."

(March 25, 1980)

(April 12, 1980)

"You can't beat the old tried and true when it comes down to the ultimate final decision...."

"Skip the birds and bees...what gives with our old-age pensions?"

(June 22, 1980)

"...and perhaps some of you wondered whose little memo started the secret pension boost plan for MPs...."

GOVERNMENT OF CANADA

(September 16, 1980)

"Mr. Humphries...dare you think of me as a wildcat?"

"But George…suppose your walkout doesn't produce the settlement you're anticipating?"

"*Roger...Dennis here thinks a burn-the-mortgage party is for when you've paid it off, not when you can't pay it.*"

(June 6, 1981)

"...We didn't have this tomfoolery before they invented postpersons"

THE VANCOUVER SUN (June 30, 1981)

"...Furthermore, getting the attention of the hospital's entire board of directors over a hard pillow by demanding an abortion..."

(September 12, 1981)

"Funk? Wagnalls here...about our definition of usury..."

(November 14, 1981)

"Loopholes are out...so find another legal word for it."

"...and while we are not the Smiths who won the lottery, we are recipients of a windfall increase in our old age pensions..."

NORRIS
© THE VANCOUVER SUN

(January 8, 1982)

"Dammit all...if they can't keep their promise to not make bombs, that's the last one I sell them."

"Why not peacefully and simply like us? Patriate something, bilingualize, invent a flag,
go metric, have a CRTC..."

(April 6, 1982)

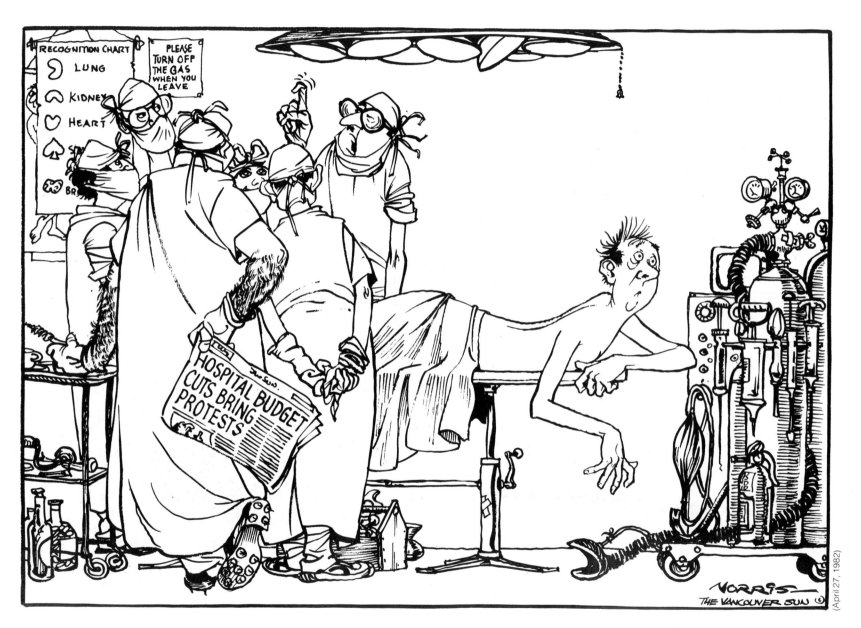

"...these cutbacks will whittle away at essentials, pare down to the bone, emasculate services, eviscerate the system..."

ADMITTING ... AL HOSPITA...

NORRIS
© THE VANCOUVER SUN

(July 13, 1982)

"We're getting a second opinion from accounting...."

(September 25, 1982)

"Dare I assume your calm demeanor is not hiding unspoken qualms over Mr. Chrétien's investment in Dome on our behalf?"

"...it now works out that you have a little too much income for welfare and not quite enough for teeth."

(September 31, 1982)

(December 27, 1982)

''As we anticipated...the Emperor has just made his Mercedes sports car a Senator.''

"You and your 'give me five good old gallons' right in front of the Men from Metric."

"I hear you've separated from that Western separatist party."

(April 26, 1983)

"…and I've come to plant that little germ of doubt in the wisdom of your choice."

"Ethel, when the world is being swamped with things protest-worthy..."

NORRIE
© THE VANCOUVER SUN

(July 5, 1983)

NEWS ITEM: FEDERAL GOV'T WOULD FINANCE 52 MEMBER 'NATIONAL PRESS COUNCIL' TO MONITOR NEWSPAPERS

"Pass the comic section!"

"Well, Dustin, out with it...what's this brilliant new concept you're proposing we adopt...?"

(August 9, 1983)